A Glimpse Within

A collection of poems and writings

❧❧

Text Copyright © 2007 by Heidi Grolemund

ISBN 978-0-6151-6588-2

Special Thanks go to:

My Mom- thank you for your love and
support. I'm glad you are my mom!

Tracy F., Mark P., Jim K. and Marie G-
thank you for your friendship and
kindness. You have all helped me a great
deal, through everything.

I love you all!

Table of Contents:

- Close Your Eyes
- Don't Open the Door
- Trust No One
- Love Lies
- Time
- I Didn't Think it Through
- What Do You Say?
- Into The Woods
- Change The Past
- I Love You Because
- A Love So Strong
- Between Us
- What Is It?
- Don't Look Away
- I
- Cats
- Breasts
- A Tear
- Iris
- OCD
- Sock
- Tessa
- A Rose
- TiKi
- Tail
- Tea'

Every Night with You

A laugh, a smile, a gleam of an eye,
As I sit next to you, I let out a sigh.
Your touch, your smell, your leg touching
mine,
The rough exterior when you couldn't be more
kind.
My heart skips a beat on this warm summer
night,
It couldn't be more perfect if I had planned it
just right.
If this is a dream I hope I never wake up,
Because, every night with you just isn't
enough.
My legs are all tingly, I can't even stand,
But I'll do anything if you just hold my hand.
This feeling of power that you hold over me,
My falling in your spell just shouldn't be.
Yet I melt at the sound of your voice,
And funny enough, it is entirely my choice.
I giggle, I smile, and my eyes fill with tears,
I'm happier than I have been in years.
If this is a dream I hope I never wake up,
Because, every night with you just isn't
enough.

His face

I long to see his face
And with my fingers, I trace
The outline of his lips
Prepared for my kiss
I long to feel his hand
On my cheek as we stand
Face to face
I long to look into his eyes
They are the truth, they never lie
I long to rest my head on his chest
And hear his heart beat in my ear
I long to just stare
As I run my fingers through his hair
I long to smell his skin
The scent of what makes him "him"
I long to feel his face
Soft and smooth after a shave
Or rough from days he missed
I long to smell the sweetness
Of my perfume on him
I long to feel his strength
As he holds me tight in his arms
I long to feel his face
And with my fingers, I trace

<u>Dreams</u>

A love never lived
A love to be lost
A person I believed
I would have at any cost
Dream after dream
Time after time
I always wished for him
I wanted him to be mine
I smile when his name I call
Although he never knew
And I left myself open for a fall
When I dreamt he loved me too
A tear streamed down my face
As I watched him from beyond
Salt on my lips I taste
Where his kiss I wished I'd found
I don't know who I'll be
When the time comes to part
He, who I'll not be able to see,
And the ache comes into my heart
From afar I watched him be
The man I wished to love
The man I wished for me
And without his love, I'd come undone

And even though it doesn't exist
The love I wish he'd give
Without him around I will miss
His eyes, his smile, the breath for which I live
Who am I, if not his love?
For I live when the dreams came
Where will I be when I must leave?
I love with my entire soul
This man who I barely know
Even though when the truth is told
He was never mine, it's true
Fiction, unrealistic fantasy
Kept me going day to day
Hoping someday it would be
And now the time comes when I can't stay
Ours path will no longer cross
I can no longer watch him everyday
And without him I'll be lost
Where do I go, what do I say?
When the time comes to say goodbye
The dream will end for good
Should the feeling I felt still hide
Or do I tell what is true
Do you know how much I love you?

I Need to Feel

I need to feel love
The love of a friend
I need to feel touch
His touch on my skin
I need to feel his soul
The soul I feel within
I need to feel whole
With him by my side
I need to hear his heart
To make me feel alive
I need to taste his kiss
His soft lips on mine
I need to smell his cologne
The scent of him near
I need to feel love
So I won't feel alone

Dream world

Blue, Quiet
Happy, Peaceful
Magical, Mysterious
Empty, Alone
Flying, Floating
Swinging, Running
Free, Painless
Gentle, White
Whimsical, Colorful
Bright and Content,
Dark and Upset
Musical, Imaginary
Ecstasy, Fantasy
Dazed

The Wall

I love you with all my heart.
I've loved you from the very start.
The many days we laugh and talk,
Sometimes I even watch you walk...
...Towards me or past me.
I think about what you might think.
I think about what you see
When you are looking at me.
I watch your eyes.
I stare at your face.
I study your every feature
And I dream about our future
But that is the problem
There is no future for us because of
The Wall
The wall that separates me from you
Even though we are friends.
We enjoy the time we spend
And the conversations we share.
We can see and hear each other
I can even smell your cologne.
But when I come too close
That is when I hit
The Wall

The wall that separates me from you.
For there is no US.
And there will never be an US.
My love for you will stay within
My heart and my soul.
And when we speak
It is a secret that I must keep
Behind the wall that separates us.

The Story of Noah

In a time of life
Where people would fight
And sinners would not forgive
A man named Noah lived
He went to the people
And told them of God's will
He encouraged them to seek Him
The people did not care
Noah told God of whom to spare
And God set forth the waters
If the people continued their ways
Then God could not permit them to stay
They would never seek God
And he could not let that go on
Noah prepared
And took in pairs
Plants and animals with him
And after the flood
The ark landed abroad
And Noah whose life was forever
Started new
With his crew
A new world
Where he would follow God's rule

Icarus Recreated

He had the need
Whatever that may be
To go higher than he should
Father asked if he understood
And he said, "Yes, don't go too far"
That night he looked at the stars
And he wondered what it was like
Now too high up in the sky
He flew into the night
His father said it wasn't right
He would never make it at that height
His wings were too small
And the pressure too powerful
At that height he will fall
To the ground and to his death
But the boy didn't hear what was said
He wanted too much and knew too little
He flew up high and the plane started to
shake
The wings broke apart and he went down
To the ground
He needed to feel or prove to himself
But now it's too late
Because he is
DEAD

I Cry Too

I don't know you, but I cry too
I feel the hurt everyone's gone through
I cry for the sadness and the loss
The tears and pain your death has caused
I say, "why was it you that had to go
With all the people who loved you so"
All the good and unselfish acts
Won't bring two little girls Daddy back
I don't know you, but I cry too
I think about why this had to happen to you
Your time should not have been through
You had so much to offer and so much to do
A life that was taken way too soon from the
start
Has left a hole in many people's heart
All of which cannot believe it's true
I never knew you, but I cry too

Midnight Music

Midnight music surrounds the night
With every chirp and every sound
You gaze around
But nothing's in sight
As midnight music surrounds the night
The water is still and the wind is quiet
The moon is full and intended just right
Midnight music, loud and clear
Will fill the earth with certain cheer
Each creature has a muse to make
While the moon and stars dance with the lake
Midnight music peaceful and soft
But at dawn
The music in gone
As the sun rises high in the sky
They bid a farewell and a goodbye
The moon and stars and others too
To midnight music that once performed the
night through

A Single Star

A single star in an evening sky,
The first one out as the days light dies
From a childhood poem,
The first night's star is for a wish
A wish I may, I might
But the poor little star is over wished
As every eye that looks in the sky
Makes a wish for the night
A single star in an evening sky
As the days light dies
Lonely and overworked, wishes for another
star
Because reflecting in the water below
He sees the first star of the night
And wishes a wish, I may, I might

Sunset

On a hill, the sky in front
You see a cloud blended into the sky
The sky is blue and orange
The cloud is purple and gray
The sun is setting,
Leaving the underside of thc cloud
Neon pink and orange
The light of the sun highlights the ripples in
the cloud
Glowing like a neon sign,
Brightening everything that lay beneath
The colors are in levels
As the sun lowers behind the earth
From light to dark, blue to orange
Then from blue to purple
And purple to black, till it's gone

A Sunset

What is it about a sunset?
That entangles you in a net?
You fall into a stare
Until everything is in glare.
In the power of the glow,
You can never feel low
The strength of sunsets,
A scene as beautiful as it gets.
It will grab you tight
As you watch intently at the light.
Warm reflection from its touch,
Stops those who rush
A moment of worldly peace,
As all commotion cease
When the joy of it ends,
On the sunset it depends

Sunshine

Sunshine shining bright
The whole room fills with light
The moment feels just right
You climb to the right height
You start to fill with fright
Your grip is not so tight
You take flight-
As you jump into the night

Moon Beams and Star Dreams

It paints a picture in the sky
That leads a path right to your eye
A beam of light
The moon so bright
An image so loud
The other sounds drown
The magnificent scene
The bright light of the moon beam
A fiery ring
The unbelievable thing
As lines of ray
Leave the thoughts of the day
Moon beams and star dreams
A gallantly gleam
What lies at the end?
Were there wishes to send?
Light pointing up and down, left and right
A light for every angle of the night
So many wishes, so many dreams
All that lay at the end of tonight's moon beam

Standing Alone

She's standing alone in a field
No one's around and no one hears
She closes her eyes and falls to a kneel
The light reflecting from her tears
She prays to God for a friend,
Someone to care and someone to share
The wind blows and the corn fields bend
She looks around and there he stands
He's outlined in light and extends a hand
The light reflecting from her tears
Together they walk, friends from the start
Thanking God with all her heart.

Scream

The anger inside
The pain that you hide
Spending each hour
Without any power
The emotion it seems
Makes you just scream
Scream to the night
Until it's just right
All of the hatred
And all that's been said
Filled up within you
Till there's no more to do
The emotion it seems
Makes you just scream
Scream to the night
Until it's just right
Forget all your fears
And let out your tears
Flowing like rain
Expressing your pain
The emotion it seems
Makes you just scream
Scream to the night
It's your turn to fight

If there is a God

If there is a God, Where is He hiding?
If there is a God, Why am I crying?
If there is a God, Why is he bleeding?
If there is a God, Why is she dying?

If there is a God, Why was it burnt?
If there is a God, Why did she drown?
If there is a God, Why do they hurt?
If there is a God, Why do we frown?

If there is a God, What will be done?
If there is a God, He isn't in sight
If there is a God, There's a man with a gun
If there is a God, There is still a fight

Shades of Gray

If life's like the colors
Filled in a rainbow
Her mood is in blue
And her rage is in red
All of her happiness
Are in shades of gray
The hopes of the future
Are as dark as the night
She dreams all in black
And wishes for light
To brighten her life
If life's like the colors
Filled in a rainbow
All of her happiness
Are in shades of gray

Will You

Will you take his place in my heart?
Will you give me your love from the start?
Will you hold me the way he should?
Would you be with me if you could?

Will you be the father he wasn't?
Will you do all that he doesn't?
Will you protect me from my fears?
Will you show concern for my tears?

Will you tell me when I do wrong?
But will you still show me your love in strong?
Will you protect me from the world?
Will you let me be your little girl?

Will you tell me you love me whenever you
can?
Then my love for you will never end
All I ask is for a hug now and then
And it will be the greatest gift you could send

When Dreamers Dream

Sitting out on the back porch
Or on the back of a great horse
Out on very good day
Or inside from a sky that's gray
When dreamers dream
Great things happen
A brilliant moment of silence
A song of love, a song of tolerance
Just to write something fun
Not stopping until we're done
Getting together, writing from the heart
With great friends from the start
When dreamers dream
Great things happen
A song that has crossed all the boundaries
A song that has really captured me
A song of fun at a chaotic pace
That teaches everyone something
Like "Happiness isn't getting what you want-
-Its wanting what you've got"
An extremely proud moment
From a song of inspiration
When dreamers dream
Its pure dedication
-A collection of quotes from Garth Brooks

Into The Darkness

The pain she feels inside
Gives her enough strength to cry
She has no love to her given
And she is tired of living
What's left for her to do?
She has thought it through
She wants the pain to be less
She closes her eyes and steps
-Into the darkness
With the pull of her finger
The hurt can no longer linger
The sound of her heart in her ears
A loud bang is the last sound she hears
All the pain and hurt is lost
But was it worth the cost?

Weeping Willow

Weeping willow hear me cry
People don't understand that I want to die
The pain that I feel, to them isn't real
But to me, it is all I feel
I'm supposed to be glad
For all that I have
With the problems I've caused
Its doesn't make up for all that I've lost
Weeping willow hear me cry
People just don't understand why
They pretend like nothing is wrong
They go day to day
Hoping it will go away
Sometimes it will hide
But the pain will never die
Weeping willow hear me cry

Close Your Eyes

Close your eyes
And take a look
Stop the lies
And pain it took
Breathe out slowly
Let out a tear
Forget being lonely
And forget your fears
Open your eyes
What do you see?
The pain that hides
Why should it be?
What do you need?
Someone to care
But from what we read
Life's not fair

Don't Open the Door

Don't open the door
Into your soul
Don't open your heart
To give love a start
No one will love you
Forever it's true
No one will change
It's up to you
No more crying
No more lying
No more trusting
No more nothing

Trust No one

Trust no one
No one's fair
Trust no one
No one cares
Everyone lies
Your pain unknown
Everyone lies
You're always alone
The sun has set
Everything's dark
The sun has set
Never follow your heart

Love Lies

Love lies
Love dies
Love hates
Love makes
Pain and tears
Distrust and fears
Love stills
Love kills
Love aches
Love breaks

Time

Time after time
Tear after tear
Lie after lie
Fear after fear
Hate after hate
Pain after pain
Hurt after hurt

I Didn't Think It Through

I'm hurting inside
And I've lost all my pride
I feel like part of me died
Those who have cared
In the time that we've shared
I screwed up and was unfair
I lost all that I earned
By taking what I've learned
And acted poorly in return
I was stupid in how I act
And it's too late to take it back
I strayed from the right track
In a short time
I've left it all behind
And I admit the fault to be mine
What's left for me to say or do?
I did what I wanted to
I'm sorry
I didn't think it through

What Do You Say

What do you say
When I'm sorry is too late?
What do you do
When you've pushed it too far?
Where do you go
When no one will accept you?
Who do you turn to
When no one is left?
How do you talk
When no one will listen?
How do you promise
When no one will believe you?
How do you start over
When no one is left to care?
What do you say...
When I'm sorry is too late?

Into the Woods

Into the woods you walk alone
Singing in your heart a lonely song
As you enter into the darkness
Your walk becomes long and endless
You feel inside a treasure lost
The moment of silence you entrust

A feeling of warmth and security
Overwhelms you as you peer into the city
Into the woods you walked alone
Walking as if your life unrolled
Forgetting your present mind
Everything was left behind

For a moment you slipped through time
As you crossed over that line
You walked for miles with no end
Never realizing what had been
Walking for hours straight
There seemed no reason left to hate

As you climbed the last hill on your quest
You reached the top and learned the rest
At the end of your journey you see ahead
A city of lights instead

The woods behind you dark from night
But the sky ahead filled up with light
One behind engulfed in silence and sadness
One ahead surrounded by music and
brightness

The choice is a hard one
Into the woods you walked alone
The sadness must come to an end
You chose ahead as you descend

Change the Past

You want to go back,
And change the past
You want to go back,
To when you were happiest.
You want to go back,
And change the past
Well, be my guest
Because my friend,-
-not even the best can change the past.
Many have tried to relive their life
In hopes of avoiding all the strife.
But I'm sorry to say
That even to this day
You can't change the past
And you can't go back.
You can only control the future.

I Love You Because

It is not for the outside that we see,
Yet the attraction is there.
It is for your eyes,
Not only the color and the make,
It is for what I see when I look into them,
It is for the soul I feel.
It is for your love,
Though it may not be given by you knowingly.
I feel it. I feel the caring and I love you for it.
True, your looks provoke some desire,
But the love falls deeper than that.
The feeling of happiness that overwhelms me
when we speak,
The enjoyment of hearing your laughter.
The feeling of self-worth,
When you smile and greet me.
Knowing and hoping through it all,
You can be there and bring with you the love
that I so much need
The warmth and tenderness of your hug and
touch,
The soothing power of your smile
And the most important,
The love I feel for you.

Even without it,
Just to look at you and to feel your presence,
To fall under the spell that you cast.
Along with your concern of my tears,
It is for the comforting and reassurance that I
feel.

A Love So Strong

Deep within my heart and soul
A feeling that I tightly hold
A love so strong and miles deep
Hopes and dreams that I must keep
Locked within my heart kept silent
From all of those that I must hide it
I love two people with all my heart
But I fear my love's one part
They don't feel for me the same
So I must keep my desires tame
It's not a love that's full of lust
Rather it's a love of friends I trust
Two men that showed me happiness
And gave me the laughter that I missed
They make me laugh and make me cry
But with all the differences, I ask why
Why and how I could find
Two people who are just so kind
I ache inside when we're apart
And I worry that with all my heart
They will leave me all alone
My life without them is unknown
In the end the truth is told
Of a love that I hold

These two men are my friends
And after all the rules I bend
They were still there when I needed
And their lectures they repeated
They did for me so much more
Then I can give them thanks for
I will always care for them
And my love will never end

Between Us

Between us stretches miles,
Too far for me to see.
Between us is the distance,
Farther than it should be.
Between us is the water,
Too deep for me to cross.
Between us is the heartache,
From the closeness that we lost.
Between us we shared laughter,
Happiness from the start.
Between is the distance,
Now that we're apart.
Between us we had a friendship,
Someone I could trust.
Between us is my sadness,
What will become US?

What is it?

What is it that I feel inside,
When I look into your eyes?
The feeling of love that never dies.
Wanting to hold you
My head against your chest.
Listening to your heart
Feeling your power from the start.
The strength you give
Helps me from day to day, live.
You are what makes me happy.
When I think of you,
My heart doesn't know what to do.
I love you in a way,
That is hard to say.
You are the reason I'm here today

Don't Look Away

You know I care, yet you walk away.
You know how I feel, but you won't stay.
You watch me watch you, and I watch you
watch me,
Yet I know you couldn't see how you have hurt
me.
Don't look away; it won't hide what you need
to say.
Don't turn you head, because how I feel won't
disappear.
Don't look away, because when you come
back,
When you look back, I will still care.
I can't tell you what I feel,
But I know what I feel is real.
And even though you had no way,
Of knowing that I'd love you each and
everyday,
You had a chance, to give me one last dance,
But you just walked away.
Don't look away; it won't change how I feel.
Don't ignore my pain inside, it won't ever go
away.

Don't look away, because when you come
back,
When you look back, I will still care.
Through so many years I have waited.
But my feelings for you have never faded.
I will still love you, as much, maybe more.
And even though I know you might never feel
the same,
That won't change how I feel for you.
But please, oh please, just
Don't look away

I

I'm not talented
Or well read
I can't dance or sing
And don't play a musical anything
I want to be known
For a talent I've shown
I don't have sport medals
I'm nothing special
I want to be something
Other than boring
I want to have a purpose
In this life where I exist

Cats

Cats for me
Are the greatness things

Creatures of mystery
Wild and carefree

Loving and smart
Of the purest heart

Playful and mischievous
Yet are full of trust

They listen to your secrets
And hear your regrets,

Follow your dreams and wishes
While your tears bring their kisses

Always ready to make you laugh
Or looking for a lap

There's nothing I don't like
When they need me to hold them tight

I think how lonely I would be
If I didn't have my cats with me

Breasts

Cumbersome
Objects of beauty
Source of illness
Hidden
Jokes and embarrassment
Displayed
Temptation and invitation
Muscle and fat
Silicone
Heavy
Sore
Bigger and Bigger
Or smaller and smaller
Only one
Sometimes none

A Tear

A tear for memories of the past
Brought forth by the smells of outdoors
A time of sadness and pain
A split second of air breezing by
Reliving flashbacks by a scent
A smile for memories of the past

Iris

Leaves like a fan
A long green stem
Reaching to the top
A waterfall of color
The sweet smell
A look unique
Colors in solids
Simple and subdued
Others, their colors blended
Vibrant and brilliant

OCD

Oh heavens me
I just hate having OCD
Check this, do that
It's a real pain in my ass
And the repetitions are insane
And the repetitions are a pain
Did I touch that, am I dirty?
Will my shower be done before I'm thirty?
Do you love me?
Are you sure?
But are you sure?
Yes, I know I'm insecure
You want me to go where?
But I'm not in my bubble,
I need my body double
Am I?
Is it?
Wait a minute
I need to change
And wash my hands
It should only take two hours
Why are you looking at me like that?
Stop
Don't

Just one question, no intentions to be mean
But before you kill me...
...Are you sure you're clean?

Sock

Sock
Orange, fuzzy and soft
Kitty
Tiny and mischievous

Nighttime and dark
Where is the sock?
Only she knows

Carried from room to room
A sock as long as her
Sounds of muffled mews

Kitty and sock
Kneading
Purring
Love

Tessa

Sweet Tessa kitty
How I am glad your mine
You're so pretty
I can't help but hug you all the time

A precious bundle of white fluff
Always on the go
You think you are so tough
And the world is too slow

I knew you belonged here from the start
You needing me and I needed you
I knew it deep in my heart
Everyday my love for you grew

You make me laugh every time you play
What you're chasing I'll never know
Knocking down everything in your way
My little white tornado

Your long hair and cute toe tuffs
Make you look so sweet
Even though sometimes you're too rough
Especially when you attack my feet

Adopting you was no accident
I believe you were heaven sent
So small and fragile, you needed me
Now together we live happily

A Rose

Petals mangled and chewed
Yellowed leaves
Sparse and eaten
Tiny bugs, life sustained
As death nears for the fragile rose

TiKi

Tiny tortie
Small and majestic
Big ears
Sloped nose
Short tail
Sweet kitty
Loving and sarcastic
Moody
Whiny
Green eyes
Bright
Perfectly independent
Curious
Mischievous
Life saver
Chest sleeper
Touch me not
Attitude
Pet me now
No don't
Ok do
Kneading a sock
Meowing
Secretly playing

Knocking down everything
Dainty
Concerned
Cherished and loved
A cat named Tiki

Tail

Swish, swish, swish
Back and forth
Whipping hard
Or hardly at all
The tip moving gently
Curled at the top
Thump, thump, thump
The hollow sound
As it hits the floor
Noise and wind
A cat's tail

Tea'

Here's a story about a cat
Although she's rather large
Please don't say she's fat
Because at her size she's in charge

Her belly is big and round
She's always ready for you to rub her tummy
So she simply falls to the ground
As soon as you start she looks so funny

Her fuzzy feet have extra toes
So soft and delicate
Like they're from a pussy willow
On her they're a perfect fit

Rolling and kicking at your hand
Licking and biting too
Only so much loving she can stand
Before she's off to someplace new

She's happy and playful
And always on the run
You can call her a trouble maker
But she's just looking for some fun

She always has her tail held high
Running from room to room
She runs so fast she can almost fly
With her, playtime never comes too soon

Whenever someone comes near
Her purr is always going
Loud and clear
A happy cat is what she's showing

She hugs you tight
And sucks on your collar
Her kneading is a silly sight
But I don't let her get too far
Because she can go all night

This cat I describe is my sweet kitty
I love her so much and think she's pretty
Tea' is the name I gave her
A pastel calico, whose love I treasure

Welcome To the Terry Springer Show

"Hi and welcome to; The Terry Stringer Show.
Today's guests say that they're human, but
some disagree.
Let's talk to them. First, Gilgamesh, how are
you doing today?"
"Fine Terry thanks."
"Second, we have Hamlet, Prince of Denmark,
how are you sir?"
"Pleasant, given the circumstances."
"Last, but not least, is Odysseus, thanks for
coming."
"Not a problem Terry."
"So fella's, who wants to go first?"
"I will Terry."
"Ok, Gilgamesh the floor is yours."
"Thanks. Well first off I'm part man, part God.
You see, I started out being a little rough
around the edges."

"A little?"

"Odysseus, you'll have your turn."

"Not if I beat his -BLEEP- first."

"Oh yeah, you think you can take me?"

"Fella's, please, settle down. Gilgamesh, continue."

"Yeah, well, Terry I started out a little rough but I have polished my ways. I chose to change for the better of my beliefs. For if I was to stay mean, where would I be now?"

"I see what you're saying, but what does it have to do with being human?"

"Everything, Terry. First off I learned something about myself in the process. I learned that if I believe I am human, then I am."

"Is that smell human?"

"That's it Hamlet I'm going to beat your - BLEEPING BLEEP"

"Oh yeah, maybe you should shave your back before you say you're human. -BLEEP, BLEEP, BLEEP-."

"Steve, what would I do without you as security? Uh, maybe you should go wash out that sword cut. Anyway, Gilgamesh, you were saying that you believe you're human. What do you have to back this up with?"

"Ok, well I learned the value of friendship with my best friend Enkidu, may he rest in piece. He gave me a sense of belonging and self worth. If it weren't for him being with me on my journey to make a name for myself, I probably wouldn't have gotten as far. I learned out of duty to self, that I am human. I feel, I hurt, and I need."

"Thank you Gilgamesh. Hamlet, do you have something to say, after you wounded one of my security staff?"

"Yes, Terry I do. First off, Steve, I'm sorry about the cut. But don't worry you shouldn't feel the effects of the poison for awhile. Anyway, the question at hand is what it means to be human. I am human, so what makes me one. Well, I live in a castle where my father was killed by my uncle who then married my mother. I feel angry and I want revenge. They say that I am crazy, but I know exactly what it is that I am doing. I am testing the waters. And I don't mean like Odysseus tested every women on his journey."

"Why you -BLEEEEEPPPP-."

"What's this?"

"Penelope, welcome to the show."

"Not now Terry. What is this -BLEEPING talk about you and other women?"

"Penelope, honey, I can explain."

"I don't want any of your excuses. I was home for years fighting off suitors for the man I love and here I find out you were 'testing the waters'."

"Penelope, I had to. I wanted to get home and I was tricked."

"Yeah, well Odysseus I was tricked by Gilgamesh who I was sleeping with."

"You what?"

"You heard me."

"Why don't we take a commercial –'BLEEP, BLEEP, BLEEP'- break?"

"Welcome back. Now that we have sent everyone else back stage, let's finish with what Hamlet was saying."

"Yeah, well am confused. I want to kill my uncle/stepfather but I know it is wrong. My father is dead and no one seems to care. I sometimes think of killing myself but then I am afraid of what will happen in the afterlife. I feel fear and sadness. Isn't it human to fight for what I believe in? I fought for the vengeance of my father and killed for the death of my mother. I fought Laertes because I was fighting for truth. I loved Ophelia and

didn't want her to die. That wasn't my
intention. What makes me human is
everything. Everything I have done from the
day I was born to the day I died."

"Well, thank you Hamlet, and I want to
express my sympathy for your losses. Now,
let's bring out Odysseus and talk with him."

"Yeah thanks, Terry. But first I need to kick
some -BLEEP. Hamlet you -God-BLEEP,
mother BLEEPER."

"Security! What? Steve's dead. Well, get
someone else out here. Good, now that
everything is settled. Odysseus, what do you
have to say."

"Terry, I am a great hero. I slayed the Trojans
and Cyclops and I did with my own smarts. I
did it. But Poseidon says that I wouldn't have
done it without him. And I believe that there is
some truth to it. If it weren't for the help I
received I probably wouldn't have made it
home. For me, being human is going out of my

way for the people I love; my wife Penelope
and son Telemachus. I felt threatened, so I
fought for my beliefs. I felt scared and invited
wisdom. I didn't start out with this, I learned
it. I learned a lot about myself on my journey."
"We're out of time. I want to thank my guests
for coming today. For my final thought; being
human is much more then what was
discussed today. Being human covers so many
boundaries. You learn as you go and if you
take what you've learned and apply it into
your life you will go much farther. The topic of
what make us human is a far broader
discussion then in my hour show. Being
human comes from inside, what you make
with it, is what makes you human. Thank you
and goodnight."

The Kitten and the Koi

The little kitten was full of joy
Perched on the waters edge
Fixated on a swimming Koi
New to the world outside
The little kitten had never seen such a sight
Thinking she found a new toy
The kitten sat and watched the Koi
Now and then the fish surfaced
Nose to nose she gave him a kiss
Tapping the water with her paw
Trying carefully not to fall
Around the pond the Koi swims
Curious with her as she is with him
Reaching her paw to touch his fin
Oops, SPLASH...
The kitten fell in

Through The Stone Gate

Walk through the stone gate
And enter a world void of anger and hate
A mythical land full of beauty and magic
A guided tour with the help of a stick
A special walking stick to keep you from harm
As long as you keep it the length of your arm
A world full of beauty and warmth you can feel
Too perfect a world for it to be real
Wild flowers cover the stone gate
That bloom until the day gets late
A stone bridge over a babbling stream
Too wonderful a sound for it to be a dream
A path to the forest is worth a visit
But wait the stick is insistent
It won't let me near it
What's the worst that can happen?
No harm lives in this magical land
I start into the forest and the stick leaps from
my hand
Some help he was at keeping me from harm.
I wander in deeper, my eyes fixed on a light
Its light gets brighter as the sky falls into
night
I stop with a jolt, my foot is stuck

Me without a flashlight, just my luck
As my eyes adjust to see what's got me
My legs are tangled in the branch of a tree
Wrapping around and intertwined
The branches and trees have come alive
They hold on tighter and tighter
And pull me up higher and higher
Way up in the tree, I see there were others like
me
How can we get ourselves free?
As we struggle and tug
The branches just become snug
The light I saw came from a cottage
Maybe someone can help us
So I scream and I shout
For someone to cut us out
Oh joy, they heard me, someone's on the way
An old lady is here and begins to say,
"If I could help you I would"
"I know that I should"
"But the keeper of the forest would be mad"
"He's big and scary and not of this land"
"What he says is what goes"
She left just like that
Slinked just like a cat
We thought it was over, no more could be
done

When through the forest, light from the sun
The branches grew limp and we were released
One by one each person down
It was good to be one the ground
But why and how did we become free
"It was me", said the stick
"I set you free"
"The beast put a spell on me"
"This was the first time since that horrible
night"
"I was a boy walking through to a light"
"I tripped over a branch and gave it a kick"
"For that he made me into a stick"
"I was to protect you but I was afraid"
"Once I overcame my fear, I could come to
your aid"
He apologized and guided our way
Back to the place we started our day
Everyone left, but I couldn't go
"What will become of you, do you know?"
"I guess I will stay forever a stick"
"Live in this world full of magic"
"It's not a bad place, you see"
"Too bad you can't remain here with me"

I smiled and thought how nice it would be
To live here with magic and mystery
"Ok, I'll stay"; I said with a smile
"But only for a little while"
So together we walked within the stone gate
In a mythical world, never knowing our fate.

Shadows

Alone in the house, two kids watched TV. It is night and their parents said they would only be gone a couple of hours. They were brothers, Ethan, 10 and Brighton, 12. It was not the first time they were left alone but the first time they were alone at night. The wind outside was strong and every time it blew a branch into the window they jumped. Brighton would punch Ethan in the arm, trying to act tough. They would never admit it but they both were scared.

As the movie was ending, lights started to flicker. A few minutes later they were out completely. Ethan started to cry. Brighton wanted to as well, but being older he felt he needed to take charge.

"Ethan, go to the kitchen and find some flashlights."

"Bright, I'm scared."

"Just go, they're in the kitchen drawer."

"I'll call next door to see if Mrs. Jenson can come over."

Ethan felt his way along the walls into the kitchen, and Brighton went to the phone. It was dead. He looked outside and saw that the neighbor's lights were still on. He remembered what his dad said about the fuse box in the basement. Maybe a fuse was blown. He shouted to Ethan to bring in the flashlights. Ethan didn't answer.

"Ethan, get in here with those flashlights. Ethan? Where the hell are you?"

Ethan came in empty handed.

"Bright, they don't work; I looked for batteries but couldn't find any."

"Shit, we used all the batteries on that race car."

"Can't we take them out?"

"Yeah, if we didn't loan the car to Matt."

"Ok, Ethan you stay here I'll go next door and borrow some from Mrs. Jenson."

It was hard for Brighton, he was scared but being older, he felt he had to be responsible and take charge of the situation. As he was heading to the front door, Ethan bumped into him.

"Jesus man, you scared me."

In amazement, Ethan said, "You're scared?"

"Hell yeah, I get scared too." Then he punched Ethan in the arm. "If you ever tell anyone, I beat the crap out of you. Now stay put."

Rubbing his arm, Ethan headed over to the couch. Brighton opened the front door and screamed. He slammed it and ran to the couch.

"Shit, shit, shit. I saw something out there."

"What?"

"I don't know? It looked like some big guy."

"Did you see his face? Maybe it was Mr. Jenson."

"No, I only saw his shadow."

The moon was full that night and everything cast shadows. Ethan tried to convince Brighton that it was something other then a murdering psychopath.

Brighton always exaggerated. Suddenly something walked in front of the window and this time the both saw it. Brighton ran and closed the curtains.

Ethan keep repeating, "we're gonna die, we're gonna die."

"Stop that, it's gonna be ok. We'll go upstairs and lock ourselves in mom and dads room. If there is someone, I know where dad keeps a gun."

"Dad has a gun?"

"Yeah, I saw him cleaning it. Man he almost blew his top. Gave me a lecture about never touching it, but this has got to be an exception."

As they headed up the stairs they saw another shadowy figure, but this time by the kitchen doorway. Screaming they run up stairs and into their parents room. Slamming the door behind them, Brighton ran straight to the closet and reached for the metal lock box on the top shelf. He was able to get it but not without bringing down everything on the shelf. The sound of the crash was loud. Then he went into his dad's underwear drawer and got the key and the bullets. As he was putting the bullets into the gun, Ethan opened the bedroom door and looked out. Brighton screamed, "Close it and put a chair under the door knob." Ethan didn't respond. Brighton went over and pulled him away and slammed the door. Ethan was shaking," I saw something coming down the hall."
"Did you see who it was?"
"No, it just looked like a shadow."

As Brighton went to push the dresser in front of the door to block it, the knob started to turn. Slowly it opened, but nothing was there. Brighton looked down the hallway, "it's clear, let's get out of here." But as he started for the door he was pushed back with force. Something pushed him so hard he fell backwards.

A shadowy figure came at Brighton. Ethan screamed and the shadow changed his direction towards him. Brighton grabbed the gun with both hands and shot at the shadow. He shouted, "Get away from him." Ethan screamed again, than was silent. The figure came towards Brighton. He shot the gun again and again until all the bullets were gone. With a last attempt, he threw the gun at the shadow. It went right through it and hit the wall. As Brighton edged back to the closet, he could feel the life being sucked right out of him.

The boy's parents came home. All the lights were on and nothing seemed out of place. Dad said, "Either they didn't have a party or they did a really good job of cleaning up."

"10 pm on a Friday night, don't tell me they're in bed already", said Mom. Then she loudly she said, "Boys, we're home." No answer. Mom started upstairs to check their room. It was untouched. She went into the master bedroom and started screaming. Dad ran upstairs to see what was wrong. The room was a mess, the shelf in the closet pulled down, bullet holes in the wall, his gun in the hallway and... the shadows of two young boys on the wall.

On a Swing

Swinging high
To reach the sky
Dreaming that you can fly
Up and down
Feet barely touch the ground
Wind blowing your hair
You without care
Back and forth
Please push me more
I need to go high
My space shuttle to the sky
It's no longer a swing
It's whatever you can dream

My Garden

The morning sun is still low in the sky. When the light reflexes off the dew, it is the perfect time to go to my garden.

The best time is early spring. Walking barefoot though the moisture kissed grass to the garden with the white picket fence. Tulips, daffodils, hyacinths, and daisies are some of my favorite spring time flowers. Roses, irises, pansies, and sunflowers are some of the others that are in my garden.

I like spring the best because it's not too cold and I can sit on the bench I keep in my garden.

Small stepping stones let me walk around without touching the ground. I wish you could see the way I see my garden.

It captures each of your senses; the smell of the fragrant petals, the sight of the colors, all the colors of the rainbow, the touch of the soft soil and the sound of the wind chimes that hang in a tree.

When I am not there, my flowers are not alone. The birds and the squirrels take advantage of the food I leave for them.

Butterflies and ladybugs also visit my garden. It's better in the spring. Summer days get too hot, drying the soil and the air. Spring has moisture and rain, drops collect on the leaves and petals, making the flowers sparkle.

The sky seems bluer and the air smells fresher and the flowers seem happier in my garden.

Demons Within

Princess Azure lay in her bed thinking of what it would be like to be dead. She didn't feel there was any reason for her to live. The emotional pain that she suffered was too much for her to take. She just wanted to die, and end all her pain. She fell asleep with the candle at the end of her bed still lit.

Darkness surrounded her, all but the light that flickered like a flame, down in front of her. She didn't know where she was or how she had gotten here. A cold chill was sent down her spine. She shivered from the fear. Her teeth chattered as she looked around. She was still wearing her nightgown. The tunnel was black and the walls and floor were made of earth. She started to walk toward the light, but she didn't seem to get any closer to it. The light just stayed where it was, and Princess Azure kept walking.

"Stop, you mustn't proceed." The beast stepped in front of her. He was massive and covered with matted hair. Princess Azure was taken aback, her heart pumping so hard that it felt as if it was in her throat. Princess Azure fearing for her life spoke to it, "Why? Where am I?" The beast just starred at her then walked away with a grin on its face. "Hey come back, where am I going?" Azure pleaded with the beast but he just vanished. Princess Azure started walking and suddenly something shined in her eye. She knelt down, and buried in the dirt floor was a sword. She picked it up and brushed it off. She kept it with her at her side, yet she didn't feel any safer.

Ahead the light went out and she stood in total darkness. In front of her appeared a giant creature lurching toward her with its many arms swinging. He was illuminated by a mysterious green light. She turned and started to run but she hit a wall of dirt. The entrance she had arrived from no longer existed. Princess Azure turned back and the creature just stood there swinging at her. He had no face, yet eyes that glowed with an eerie red light. She cowered against the wall. Suddenly she felt a searing pain in her arm. She could feel the warmth of her own blood dripping off her. It finally dawned on her to use the sword. She glanced down and saw the sword in her hand. She lifted it up and swung with all her might at the creature. It let out an ear-piercing scream and then disappeared into the darkness.

Blackness still enclosing her, Princess Azure started walking down the hall. She was confused and frightened. She had no idea of where she was and if she would make it out alive. She was deep in her thoughts and fears when in front of her jumped a two headed monster full of hair and a smell that repulsed her. She couldn't breathe with the odor but the monster kept getting closer and closer. She backed up as it approached but the wall behind her closed up again and she walked into it. She started to choke as the monster sucked the breath right out of her. She fell to her knees gasping for air. With what little energy she had left, she swung the sword at it. The monster's two heads fell off and rolled next to her as she slowly caught her breath. The monster and its heads shriveled up until they were no more.

Princess Azure slowly stood up. She continued her travels weakened and afraid. The wall was the only thing keeping her from falling to the ground as she leaned against it for balance. A dim light appeared at the end of the tunnel.

Without warning there stood a demon, with horns and fire everywhere. The flames engulfed Princess Azure and she screamed as they attacked her, burning her entire body. She swung the sword in hopes of killing it but the flames and heat were so intense that they just turned the sword a hot, glowing red. She dropped the sword instantly and felt completely powerless. She fought as much as she could but had nothing left of herself to give. No more strength and no willpower left. She thought it would be easier to just die than fight. The demon spoke, "I knew you would be mine. You are nothing and will never be anything. You shouldn't have even tried to fight me. This is my world, where you will die a slow and painful death. The more you fight the worse you will be." Princess Azure quietly said, "But why? Why am I here?" "You are here because you wanted to be," replied the demon. He continued, "You thought of dying and killing yourself because of the pain you had to endure. Now you are mine, you willed yourself to me."

Princess Azure looked at her bleeding and burned body. She was badly hurt and believed that there was nothing left to do.

Then she thought, this beast was too confident and she would not allow herself to give into this demon. No fire would stop her. She would not allow herself to die this way. She held her breath and ran as fast as she could towards the light that shined through the flames of the demon. She had done it. The fire was gone and so was the demon. She entered the light and was blinded by it. Then the blackness returned.

Princess Azure woke up to find herself in her own bed. She remembered the dream as though it was real. She stood up and found herself bleeding and bruised. She hurt all over and was very weak. Yet her soul had felt free. She had battled the demons within.

Secret

There's a secret that I hide
Something I do and I don't know why
Not too many people know
But I'm afraid it's starting to show

I pull out my hair to relieve stress
Hair on my head and face is the best
I've been doing it since I was young
I just start pulling hairs one by one

I don't know why I started this
But I know that it makes me embarrassed
It's hard for people to understand
They think stopping is as easy as sitting on
my hands

It's not that easy to quit
I've tried every chance I get
Pulling out my hair calms me
It's a form of OCD

I'm not the only one with this
It's an easy illness to miss
One day I hope I can be "repaired"
So I won't have the need to pull out my hair

It may be a habit I need to break
But the emotions behind it are not fake
Even I as get older I may never be the same
Trichotillomania- is the illness that I blame

To go

I have to go
I can't stay here
I have to go
I have to disappear
I don't know why
Or for how long
Or what is driving me so wrong
I have to go
Go away
I don't know where
And why is hard to say
I have to go
There has to be a way
Why can fears drive me so
Far away
I have to go
I can't stay here
I have to disappear

What Can I Do?

Seeing the sad faces
In different places
Feeling the heartache
From the moment you wake
Wondering, as I think it through
Wishing there was something I could do
Hoping there was something I could say
To make you smile and brighten your day
Listening to what is on your mind
And hoping all your problems could be left
behind
Wondering, as I think it through
Wishing there was something I could do
Some way to make you feel better
And to once again, hear your laughter
I don't know why you are so unhappy
Just tell, me what can I do?

What Words Can Do

I'm skeptical of everyone
I even am of you.
I really want to trust someone
But I just wouldn't know who.
You say you are my friend
That you'll help me, but you lied.
Because when I really needed you
You go and pass me by.
I don't know if you really care
And I know you don't understand.
Are you just throwing words everywhere?
There's an impact that you put on me
When you say you want to help.
Deep within me, farther than you can see.
You tell me that you'll be there
Then I call you and you tell me there's nothing
you can do.
And to me it's just not fair.
If you're going to say something
You better follow it through.
You don't know what your words can do.
Sometimes I just need someone
You don't need to say the magic words.
But when I feel bad, I just cannot be alone.

It's not always going to be this way
I know that things will change.
That you can't be with me each and everyday.
The most important thing I want from you
Is for you to tell the truth.
That's the best thing you can do.
You tell me you are my friend.
You tell me you want to help.
But then you decide you can't help me in the
end.
I know you can't give me the help that I need.
I don't expect more from you then you can
give.
But I do expect honesty.
I need friends more than anything.
So when you're nice to me
I tend to believe everything you say.
If you are going to say something
You better follow through.
Because you can't imagine what your words
can do.

Forever Happy

Once upon a time, in a small village lived a little girl. She lived with her family and many pets. The little girl lived a happy life. Everyday, rain or shine, the little girl skipped around the village, picking wildflowers. Sometimes she would go to the park and climb and swing. She would have so much fun. She would stop and talk with the animals; they never talked back, but she still understood them. Everything she heard sounded like music; the wind in the trees, the birds chirping, even the cars driving by.

With each year, the little girl grew older. One day, she realized that she was no longer a little girl, she was grown up. Everything she once did; walking in the rain, swinging and climbing were no longer appropriate. The once happy little girl was no longer a happy little girl. There were rules and expectations to follow. For a while she did all that she was supposed to but she came to find out that it was no fun. So she went back to being the happy little girl she once was. She was looked down upon and called immature. So one sunny day she went for a walk. She picked wildflowers and stopped at the park to climb and swing. She sat in the grass and listened to the birds and the wind. She smiled at the sky remembering how she was once a happy little girl who lived in a small village. She reached into her bag and closed her eyes. She was forever going to be the happy little girl she once was.

Once upon a time in a small village there lived a little girl. She lived in a small cemetery with wildflowers and animals all round.

Can you feel it?

Can you feel it; can you hear it or see it? It's there. Look hard, can you see the pain? Of course not. You can only see what you want to see. If you listen carefully, you can hear the crying, you can feel the pain and you can see the anger. If you try hard enough, you can feel it, but you don't want to. You won't admit the truth. The pain, the sadness, and the crying.

Look inside past the anger and the fear, look hard and you'll see it, the hurt. No one knows why it's here, but it is and it won't go away. It just gets bigger. It hurts. Can't you hear me cry, can't you feel my pain, and can't you see me hurt? Why won't it go away? Make it go away. Am I the only one who can hear, feel and see it?

Listen. Empty everything from your mind. Close your eyes, open your soul, look deep inside yourself. Listen. Can't you hear the crying? It's all that I hear. The pain, the sadness, fear and anger. It's here, it hurts. Help make it go away, make it go away. Why can't you see it? Why can't you feel or hear it?

Why won't it go away? Why does it keep getting bigger? It hurts and crying won't help, nothing will make it go away.

Can't anyone see it? ...Open you eyes, look closely. Do you see anything? Listen, do you hear anything? Where's the crying? The crying is gone. Silence. It's quiet, where's the heartbeat? I'm scared...

Who am I?

Who am I?
Where do I belong?
Where am I going?
And where am I from?
What am I doing?
Why am I here?
What is the reason I'm hiding in fear?
I don't understand.
I'm not quite too sure.
I feel like I'm falling
And can't reach your hand.
But how do I know that you're holding your
hand out?
Maybe you don't care or you can't hear me
shout.
Are you against me?
Am I always in your way?
I'm tired of crying.
I'm tired of not know what comes each day.
Who am I?
Where do I belong?
I feel young and I feel old
I feel that I am lost.
Things move so fast.

I can't grab hold.
I don't want to die.
And I don't want to hurt.
But I am confused.
I think and I wonder.
What is there left to lose?
What do I have, what do I do?
I know what I want.
But do I deserve it?
I want to be happy.
I want to be loved
Do I want too much?
I know what I feel.
Fat and ugly.
Friendless and lonely.
What can I give?
To this world where I live.
Why can't I just be normal in an abnormal
world?
Why can't I fall in with the daily routine?
I want to be looked at.
I want to be seen.
I want to feel something other than pain.
I look through my eyes but nothing seems
real.
Why is it so?
Why is it this way?

Why must I go through this each and
everyday?
Who am I?
Where do I belong?
I don't know why
But everything I do is wrong.
Who am I?
Is this who I am?
I hate this person that before you stands.
I act everyday.
Just to get through it some way.
But why must it be?
I just can't see.
Why I work so hard to get to the night.
It just doesn't seem right.
To work that hard just to get up the next day
And have to do it again.
I do this for a while.
But what then?
For the rest of my life, I go this way?
What fun it that?
It's not much of a life I'd say.
I feel so much and think so much.
I see things I want.
I know what I need.
I'd be happy and feel love.
That's what I believe.

My mind works so hard that thoughts get lost.
And my emotions take over me.
But when that is controlled
I could be free.
That is when the magic would come.
And I would no longer be the only one.
I would be loved and I'd be happy.
That is what I need.
That is when I'd be free.

Rage

You breathe in and feel the rage
You hope it'll pass but it's just the first stage
You open you mouth to speak
But all that comes out is anger
To your friends you're a complete stranger
The pressure builds till you want to scream
You feel it's not real, that you're in a dream
You wonder where it came from, what brought
it on
Everyone's the enemy, everyone's wrong
It's not their fault, it's not like they should
know
Who cares what's right, whatever you say goes
When rage is in control

On the Edge

You're standing alone
Not wanting to go home
You feel lost and confused
And there's nothing left to lose
Your pain can be ended
If only a hand can be lent
There's two ways to go
You're on the edge
Of life and death
One chance is final, you know
You don't know what to do
I'M on the edge of no return
I'M ready to watch the bridges burn

Strength

Deep within, a power so strong
That keeps you moving all day long
The feeling keeps pushing you
Until all your jobs are through
Whether you're happy or not
Or when you're getting ready to stop
The feeling you possess is strength
It will take you the entire length
It helps you make it through each day
It follows you all the way
No matter how tired or frustrated you are
You have the strength and you can go far
Farther than you can imagine
It can provide you with what's needed within
The power of your strength is up to you
The willingness you have is what will pull you
through

I've been Alone

Setting: A dark semi empty room. The only light is from a TV set. Far left-hand corner, a bed slightly visible. Upper right-hand corner TV facing stage left, one chair facing TV. Four time periods, each ten years apart.

Characters: Abby, Jonah, David, Eli. Eli is the only one to age while Abby, Jonah and David appear to stay the same age. Eli Changes with every time period.

Scene 1: Eli leaves her bed in the left-hand corner of the stage and is young, around 7 years old. David, Jonah, and Abby in that order with Abby nearest to the audience, are facing the TV. Nothing is playing on the TV but static or snow. The 3 are adults in their 30's. Notice the way they are sitting. David is sitting in the chair normally, Jonah is sitting on the floor Indian style, and Abby is laying on her stomach with her right hand holding up her head. The 3 rarely, if ever move. They are in what appears to be a trance as they store into the TV. There is no known relation between the 4 characters.

Eli approaches the three with simple childlike mannerisms.
Eli: "Look David. I dressed myself today."
David, with little movement; "huh? Yah, Good."
Eli: "Jonah? See, I matched my socks this time."
Jonah not noticing breathes in. Then out.
Eli: Now discouraged, "Abby? Abigail, see all by myself."
With no response, Eli sulking walks off to her bed.
LIGHTS OUT

Scene 2: David now sits where Jonah had and Jonah is where Abby was and Abby is now in the chair. No apparent changes in behavior and the audience should not pick up on the seating change dramatically. Eli is now 17 years old, while the three have not changed in age. Eli sits on the edge of her bed fidgeting. She is still quiet and timid, with childlike mannerisms. She approaches the group.

Eli: "David, Jonah, Abby?"
Abby: Without feeling and movement, "what?"
Eli: "why do you do that?"
Abby: "do what?"
Eli: "that thing you are doing?"
Abby doesn't respond.
Eli timidly walks off to her bed.
LIGHTS OUT

Scene 3: The seating of the three has changed again in the same manner. David is now lying on the floor, Jonah in the chair, and Abby is Indian style. Eli, now 27 is still childlike, yet grown physically. She is still on her bed. The three are still in a trance in front of the TV. Eli is crying.
Eli: Walking towards them, Jonah, David, Abby? Why? Why, must you be this way? Why are you so still? I am lonely and scared."
Jonah: "Eli", with no feeling, "calm down."
David: Also with no feeling, "yes, Eli. It's ok."
Eli: "Abby say something."
Silence
Eli, head down, walks to her bed crying.
LIGHTS OUT

Scene 4 the three people are back to their original position. Eli is now 37 and she is very weak appearing, with no personality left. She approaches the three.

Eli: "I've been alone for too long. I've been unloved for too long. I can't go on like this anymore. I'm dying inside and out. Goodbye Abby, I loved you like a sister. Goodbye Jonah, I loved you like a brother. Goodbye David, I just loved you and I still love you" She kisses him gently on the lips and walks away.

Her bed is no longer visible to the audience and as Eli walks away, neither is she. A brief silence fills the room. Then the three "wake up". They blink and started to move around as if they were only there for a short time. David gets up and looks around. He notices Eli's bed was empty and untouched.

David: "Where's Eli?"
Jonah still unsure about where he was himself: "I don't know. I haven't seen her. Abby?"
Abby: "I haven't seen her either. Where could she be?"

David: "I..." about to speak, he suddenly stops. He stares at Eli's bed, and then touches his lips where Eli kissed him. A tear ran down his face.

LIGHTS OUT
END

You should've said Goodbye

I knew one day everything would change
And that things could never stay the same
I knew one day you would leave
And that you couldn't always be with me
I am very happy for you
Knowing this is what you want to do
And even though I'll miss you so
There's just one thing I need you to know
Because of you, I'm hurting inside
I really think you should've said goodbye

Strange New World

With the feeling of loneliness and worthlessness, the girl imagined what life would be life is she weren't alive. She felt she didn't want to live much longer. With that thought in her mind, she went to bed. As each moment passes, she fell into a deeper sleep. Finally, she reached the point of sleep where she started to dream.

All was dark, all except the long line that appeared in front of her. The line was so vivid that she felt she could walk right up to it and touch it. As she fell deeper into the sleep, the line got closer. She extended her arm and touched it. As she did, it moved and split open. She pulled the bottom down and inside there was a strange new world. She stuck in her head and felt she was no longer asleep in her bed. Was this it? Was the division between life and death?
She was scared.

The world was cold and lonely. There was a dim red-orange tint that lighted the strange new place. It looked as if there was no end to the world. She could walk forever and get nowhere. Was this it, was she going to die? Many thoughts went through her mind. She wondered; if she was to enter this world, would she ever return to her own life or will she be trapped in there for eternity. Half in the new world and half she in her dream, she didn't know if this was all real or that she was having a dramatically realistic dream. As she continued to scan the world, she smiled. The thought had crossed her mind to live alone in this world. Yet, she wasn't sure what to do. She could enter this place and stay forever or wake up the next day in her bed. The place was dim and dreary; the smell of old filled the air. Was this hell? Was it heaven? Or was it the space between the two?

She re-entered her dream to the darkness and then back to the new world. The dream world was safe and she knew where she was. The new world was scary, but her curiosity decided to take the chance. She entered the new world. Once she was inside, she looked around. All she saw was space, a reddish-orange space. Nothing up, down or on either side. She turned completely around and didn't see the line through which she entered. She felt around, terrified. No wall, nothing, only miles and miles of complete emptiness. What had she done? Many things raced through her mind, such as; had she trapped herself in a space between heaven and hell? Will she ever go home? Will she be lost forever in eternal loneliness?

Love Michael

Dear Jodie,

Today is October 14, 1941 at 12:30 am. Right now I'm sitting in a 3- foot deep hole in 2 feet of water. My only protection is from the tree above me, blocking the storm. I look up and see no stars through the downpour, no moonlight, nothing except darkness. I miss you so much Jodie. All I can think about is you. God, I miss you more then my freedom. God. Did you ever stop to think about that word?

God. In God We Trust. Pray to God for all our answers. In God We Trust? Damn it, Jodie. It just pisses me off. I prayed. I prayed day night and day. I prayed for the rain to stop. I prayed for the sun to shine. I prayed for the killing to stop. I prayed to God with all my heart to spare my life and the lives of all the others. In God I trusted my life, to protect me and help me make a difference. That is the whole reason I signed up to serve my country. But by the time this war is over there will be no country left, and no people left to live in it.

There are no lives left, no souls. Everything is as if we are in hell.

Five hours ago I watched as a guy, my best friend, a guy that I told could be the Godfather of our child, jump into a hole and right into an explosion. Unfortunately he didn't die right away. I say unfortunately because along with the blast, his lower body was blown off. He sat there in the water filled hole, as a leg and bones floated next to him. The water was so cold he didn't even realize they were his. I cried along with him as he found out he couldn't move. I cried with him and for him and I swore to God that I was never going to forgive Him.

Just last month a new recruit came in. An 18 year old kid, 18 years of life to be ended here. He thought he was going to make a difference. He thought that he was going to save the world, like they show in the movies. Yesterday he went crazy. His mind went numb and he just the left the world he came to save. He had seen too much blood and death and the noises were so loud. He started shaking and staring at nothing. He began to mumble and scream. They are taking him to a hospital as soon as everything settles down. Jodie, I swear to you, if I come home with my life and sanity, so help, my boy, our son will never be put through this. If I ever pray to God again, it will be to keep our son away from this hell that we call "a future for freedom". This letter may be graphic, but it's to remind us of what it is like, so that no one will make the same mistake. I love you with all my heart and as I've said before, remember me, as I will always remember you.

Love Michael

10/28/59

Dear Mama,

You know how you told me to never
make friends in the Army? Well Mama, I made
a friend. Please don't be mad, Mama. I like
him and we have a lot in common. We're the
same age and he doesn't live that far from us
in Connecticut. Oh Mama, he's the first real
friend I've ever had, and he likes me Mama, he
really likes me!
Mama, may I ask you for a favor?
Justin (that's his name), he doesn't have a
family Mama, he has nowhere to go for the
holidays. Can I bring him home for
Thanksgiving? Please Mama? Please say yes. I
love you.

Your son, Matthew

11/12/59

Dear Mama,

As you probably heard, there was an attack. Don't worry, I'm alright. We were out on our daily walks, scouting out the territory, when they hit us. Oh Mama, I was so scared. And never mind about Justin, Mama. He was killed yesterday. Oh mama, I miss him so much. They're letting us come home a week from tomorrow for Thanksgiving. Oh Mama, why did he have to die? Why Mama, why? My bottom bunk seems so empty. I'm alone again, Mama. Now I know why you told me never to make friends in the Army. I love you.

Your son, Matthew

Goodbye

There comes a time to say goodbye
And you tell yourself you mustn't cry
Your future seems all together lost
But your friendship was worth the cost
The memories inside of happy times
A feeling in your heart left behind
Times of laughing and of sharing
All characteristics that are bearing
The honesty of truth and the truth of honesty
A friend that's gone away
Not without a feeling that will stay
Reminding you that everyday
You are a better person and a friend
Because of a friendship shared in a special
way
There comes a time to say goodbye
And tell yourself you must not cry
But instead the best you can do
Is to say "goodbye" and "thank you"

Daydreaming

As I sit on the swing, I watch. I watch the sun slowly fall behind the trees. I watch the clouds float across the light blue sky. I see the birds playfully chase one another and play tag. The bees and bugs go from flower to flower. They are happy. Even the trees are happy as the gentle breeze caresses their leaves.

The sky is so peaceful and endless. I wonder what it would be like to fly carelessly around, through the air, high above everyone; with only one thought in mind- watch out for trees. I wish so much that I could fly up away from danger, to watch people who look as small as ants. To be up away from the pain. If only I could fly.

If life wasn't so complicated, I would live outside and watch the sun wake up and put in a full days work, then beckon the moon for its midnight's job. To watch as the sun drifts down behind all and as the moon floats high into the sky. To watch the stars twinkle and sparkle as the moon dances on the water. To watch as the birds, squirrels, rabbits, fish, bugs and everyone else in nature's family tree live their lives happily. The sun has begun to set slowly behind the earth and with it my daydreaming comes to an end.

Magical World

The room was magical. You could get
lost in all the imagination. All the posters and
dolls. When you're upset, you can put on
some music, turn up the volume and wish.
You can wish for things you know could never
come true. But dreaming it would was good
enough. Who knew, if you wished hard
enough, it could come true. To wish, while
looking at a poster of an Arts Festival, you
could become part of that world. To sit on the
step of a beautiful house, in a world that
seems flawless.

To look at a flower and ribbon
headpiece and become part of the Renaissance
period, with the old English way of speaking.
To wear the dresses and watch jousts. On the
other wall you stare into a poster of a Lilac
Festival and are magically on a bench
surrounded by fragrant flowers and lilacs. You
turn on the radio and you hear your favorite
singer and you believe you are at a concert
with that singer in person.

You look up, out the window and see
the stars and the moon. You dream of how

peaceful the sky is and you become part of it. High above all, looking down. You see a picture of a cottage with smoke coming out of the chimney; they sky dark with the last bit of an orange sun fading out. The sound of the brook in the yard, water falling through the rocks as it makes its way down the stream. You become the owner of this land. You live there with the deer's and unicorns and magical fairies. Ducks and swans swim in your brook and the sound of nature is all the entertainment you need.

You see a picture of an Irish countryside and are now in another country, walking the streets of Ireland. You take in all the sights you thought you would never see. You look at a calendar and are now walking through the rainforest. Standing in the middle of everything green, next to a waterfall, with unusual but beautiful bugs and animals.

You're distracted by the television. You see a show you like and are now a part of **that** world. Not the Hollywood world, but the world being portrayed, where everything that almost never happens in a lifetime, happens in 30-60 minutes. You close your eyes briefly and are in a world you don't recognize, but you're happy.

Briefly took a little longer then you thought and you wake up the next morning to reality. And even though your wish didn't come true, you live with the fact that you were dreaming. But it was some dream...

Where's My Blankie?

The days are tough
And down right rough
Sometimes I'm mad
Sometimes I'm sad
Everything will be fine with me
But first, where's my blankie?
So warm and soft
Mom just turned the dryer off
It's a comfort to me
Why can't you see?
There is something everybody needs
To make them feel good
Like everyone should
I have places to be
But first, where's my blankie?
Oh Mom, why not?
I ask in the parking lot
My security you can't abolish
Why can't I take my blankie to college?

Bath and Body Works

So many perfumes
So many gels
So many lotions
So many smells
My favorite store
I want to buy more
I spend and I spend
Until in the end
My charge card is maxed
But there is still stuff on the racks
I have to buy
I don't know why
I shop till it hurts
I just love...
Bath and Body Works

My Memoirs

My name is Joshua and I am an ant
Have you ever imagined my life?
I'll bet anything that you can't
Mine is a life that is full of strife
For every one of your steps
There are 100 of mine
You walk by us and no one is left
You think we're just fine
Well guess what? We aren't
The life of an ant is a hard one
As much as we try
We can't get anything done
And would you like to know why?
Because of you, can't you see?
Trade lives with me
For just one day
And I know that you will say
"The life of an ant can't be beat"
Have you ever seen from an ants view,
The size of your FEET?

My Soul Mate

The one that I love
The one I dream of
The perfect date
He is my soul mate
He is the best
Above all the rest
Funny and smart
And that's just the start
Handsome and cool
Sometimes the fool
It's honest to say
That he is my soul mate
Together we are one
And we have so much fun
Joking and games
We tend to think the same
I hate when we are separate
Since he IS my soul mate
He doesn't know
I would never let my feelings show
Together we would have the perfect life...
But what would I do about his wife?

Summers Run

Look up right now
And you will see
The bluest sky that could ever be
Not even the smallest cloud
Look at the trees
As the gentle warm breeze
Blows lightly against the leaves
Look at the birds
The prettiest sounds you've ever heard
The big ones and little ones
Soaking up all the warm sun
Each one singing along
There in the garden, the flowers grow
Pink, orange, yellow, and purple, you know
Just about every color of the rainbow
Take a deep breath and smell all the smells
Roses and irises, sunflower and bluebells
Close your eyes and feel the sun
The warm winds of summers run
All the sights, the sounds, the smells as well
There's just one thing that bothers me
It's all those pesky bees

My Favorite Winter Memory

I was young, a little girl
I was small and it was a big world
I sat in the family room
It was to be bedtime soon
The night sky was pitch black
As black as my cat
The snow fell lightly
And laid upon the ground brightly
Because of the light from the wall
It made it the perfect snow fall
Each flake rested on the snow
That fell a couple days ago
It sparkled and twinkled
Like diamond and crystal sprinkles
The snow was so bright
Even at night
My sisters and I could not resist
To my Mom we had to insist
We had to go out and play
You don't get a snowfall like this everyday
Our snowsuits on
We were out in a bound
We didn't really play
I think we just stayed

Watching the snow land
It was too perfect to ruin
So beautiful I remember
A flawless night to me
It was my favorite winter memory

Christmastime at the Mall

It's nearing that time
Just when you thought all was fine
You go to the store
You open the door
And you stare in awe
It's Christmastime at the mall
The decorations and toys
The whole place filled with noise
People packed in
Bags up to their chin
Pushing and shoving
Your head is throbbing
It's only November
There was a time you remember
Christmas didn't begin this soon
Next year why not start in June?
The shopping, the stress
I don't have a dress
Oh no, nature calls
Not when it's Christmastime in the mall
The line extends out the door
It's practically in the next store
Gross, yuck, and there's only one stall
I hate Christmastime at the mall

Gift wrapping, spend more
Sales in every store
Ripping and grabbing
One sweater's worth having
50 dollars, you're joking?
Hey, that's my side you're poking
I'm out of here
A time full of cheer?
A warning for the end of fall
Oh lord; it's Christmastime at the mall

Princess Amber
-For Amy & Troy

"Princess Amber"
"Princess Amber"
Night and day
It's "Princess Amber"

Open a can
And fill my dish
Clean my litter pan
Give me a kiss

Give me my supper
And I'll eat every bite
I search the whole house
For a spot that's just right
And for all of your love
I throw up on your rug

Someone's at the door
I barely land on the floor
Daddy's home, it's time to play
Because Mom's done nothing but work all day

Sliding, flying jumping around

Daddy catches me before I hit the ground
Oh no, watch out! I want my Mom
Meow, meow, I want her now

My favorite spot
The window sill
My friend the bunny
So quiet and still
He hops and plays
But he cannot stay

It's finally time to go to bed
The inbox looks nice
It's stuff Mom hasn't read

Well bye for now
Thanks for sharing my day
My name is Princess Amber
As you can see
Things always go my way
But how else should I act?
After all, I AM a cat

Meeka Kitten

My baby number two
How I am really going to miss you
I loved you so
I wish I didn't have to let you go
My angel in fur
So loudly you purred
A love so genuine
I was glad you were mine
Perfect and sweet
From your nose to your fuzzy feet
I wish you could have stayed
I'm sorry it didn't work that way
I'm sorry for what I put you through
I know it wasn't fair to you
How I wish you were snuggled on my chest
Where you loved to sit and rest
You were playful and fun
A loving little one
I will always cherish you
And just remember
Your first mommy loved you

The Feelings

Feelings boiling up inside
Not knowing if I want to scream or cry
Frustrated more than you know
The feelings just continue to grow
Not knowing the exact reason
And it has nothing to do with the changing
season
Stress and pressure just builds up
And I want to scream "that's enough"
But I can't, I'm overpowered
So strong, nothing else can be heard
I know the feeling, like old friends
But not good and comforting in the end
More like an enemy that just stopped by
I can't really pinpoint the reason why
How can I send the feelings away?
Because I really don't want them to stay
The anger and sadness, frustration and stress
So many emotions, no time to rest
I want to scream, I want to cry
I want these feelings to go away and die
So I can live normally again
But I'm not sure exactly when
When will I have happier days?

It is really hard to say
I hate feelings like this
Happiness is something I definitely miss

Better Days

Better days ahead
Well, that's what they said
I didn't believe it
I figured the pain would never quit
I would always carry a cloud of gray
But slowly it happened...
Better days
The sadness lifted
And away the clouds drifted
The sun began to shine brighter
The weight of my pain got lighter
Frowns became smiles for...
Better days
Good things were happening
Who would have thought
There would be...
Better days?
I was so sad
And everything was going bad
I never imagined all that could be
The depression faded
And I would be free
Free from the sadness and the hurt
Being buried alive, covered in dirt

That's how I felt most of the time
I never believed there could be...
Better days
Now I am happy
As best I can be
Things will never be perfect
I know they can't be
But I smile and laugh more now
And try my best, the best I know how
My world looks clearer
And I see the good in things I'm near
I'm just glad I can say
That I have got... Better days

Walking Alone

Walking alone
No one to know
How I feel
I'm in this myself
With no one to help
I'm walking alone
Humming a song
With one thing in mind
How I'm hurting inside
The people I see
Look right through me
Not noticing anything
Shallow and wrong
I'm just not that strong
To let it roll off my back
Why don't they know?
Doesn't it show?
All that I'm looking for
Is just one foot in the door
All it would take
Is one little hello
For my smile to show
But no, that's not what you do
When I walk up to you

You wave me away
With your smile so fake
It cuts like a knife
This is some life
Here on my own
Walking alone

Alone in a Crowd

I am there
They look right through me
I speak
They don't hear me
I know I'm there
They don't care
I'm alone in a crowd
I cry
They don't see the tears
I laugh
It falls on deaf ears
I try to join in
It's like I am invisible
I'm alone in a crowd
They talk like I'm not there
I ask a question
I get a blank stare
I could fall
And they would not catch me
They continue with their lives
As if I don't exist
How can I live like this?
Each time I'm around
The smaller I feel

The more my world feels surreal
If they don't see me or hear me
Maybe I'm not here at all
That's why I feel...
Alone in a crowd

I Wonder

Sometimes I wonder. I wonder if you are a coward and never cared. I wonder if you cared too much. I wonder if I am supposed to hate you, or if I am supposed to thank you. I wonder if you have failed me, or if I failed myself. I wonder if you could have ever helped me, or I was supposed to help myself. I wonder if you gave me something, or if you took something away. I wonder if I would have made it or if I would have failed if I stayed. I wonder whether something had been accomplished or if it was a waste of time. I wonder if I needed you as much as I did or if you gave me more than I needed. I wonder if I should forgive you or ask you to forgive me. I wonder if I should worry about the past or if you worry about me.

Not Who You Thought

When you look at me
It's not the real me that you see
I am who people want me to be
I fit into the world around me
I'm full of secrets
And many regrets
Hidden pain
And hidden shame
I want to be liked
So I act just right
The truth will never show
The real me you'll never know
Because, if the real me before you stands
I'm positive you wouldn't like who I really am

9/11/2001

Today history has changed
Our lives as we know it, rearranged
Thousands of people were hurt and killed
Death and terror at one person's will
We will always remember September 11
And pray to God that there is a heaven
Our safety was threatened
When we were attacked
Now our awareness was heightened
By one horrid act
What was the reason?
Why did this happen?
The poor passengers and flight captain
The buildings occupants and innocent, all
pleading
Why did people have to die?
Destruction and ruins in the street lie
So many lives ended
Can America ever be mended?
Although the repairs have started
America will never be the same
How can we forget those hollow hearted
Who began this war game?

We will rebuild, though the memories will
remain
The wounded, the dead, what was to gain?
Americans pulled together
The lives lost will be remembered
We saw heroes in all
Firefighters, police, all involved
Showed courage and bravery
And amiss the danger, stood tall
Many people owe them their lives
And a tremendous thanks from us all
If good comes from bad
Good would be the togetherness we had
They may think they have broken us
But they actually strengthened us
For now we will fight
We will bring the evil doers down
And again one day
We will feel secure and safe
But we will never let down our guard
To destroy us now will be twice as hard
United We Stand
We will not end
We will survive
Until you are caught
"Dead or alive"

A Hero Remembered- Dale Earnhardt

What happened on that fateful day,
In peoples minds will forever stay
What makes a hero differs for all
They may even put you on a pedestal
You were strong, and true in your heart
You made them love you from the start
They fulfilled their adventures vicariously
through you
Their lives strengthen by what you do
Now they sit in shock by the news
For many, they still can't believe it is true
You were invincible from harm
Nothing you could do was wrong
But reality has spoken that you are gone
You weren't supposed to die at all
You were a hero to the big and small
But now your flag stands at half mass
People are waiting for the hurt to pass
Many did not know you much
Never even watched you race or lift a clutch
But your name was everywhere
You wouldn't believe how many people cared
Whether they were NASCAR fans
Or just an ordinary everyday man

They knew who you were and what you were
about
They knew you were kind without a doubt
The shock still lingers around the world
The news by now, everyone must have heard
A legend to many, one fatal mistake
Everyone knew of the chances you'd take
Now as we sit and wonder in disbelief
Hoping beyond hope, that it was untrue
That you are not gone
How can someone in an instant, just die?
So many people are asking themselves why
But the truth will set in eventually
The news will be shown repeatedly
For now we must go on the way we were
While in the back of our minds, we keep...

A hero remembered

To Love Someone

Have you ever loved somebody so much it
makes you cry?
Feeling like a part of you dies inside
That's how I feel when I look into his eyes
As the tears well up in mine
Everyday you hope and pray
That you'd be with him one day
But the love is so strong that you stay away
Just to see him and be near him
Puts your body in a spin
Till your heart is twisted inside
And it makes you want to cry
Has there ever been someone you needed to
the highest degree
That it scares you inside because you thought
"I only need me"
You've never felt love like this
It's a feeling you don't want to miss
Just to see his face looking right at you
He probably doesn't feel the same way you do
And the tears well up inside
Has there ever been a time when you say "he's
not mine"
That everything will not be fine

Because without him you feel so lost
That love came with a cost
You hope you can love another in time
But the tears still well up inside

Behind The Door

Morning is here and she wakes up crying
She's not ready to face another day even
though she is trying
The sun is out and the wind's in the trees
She feels the pain in everything she sees
Everyone says it will get better in time
So she tells everyone she is fine
They don't understand and it's easier to lie
It's better if people didn't know she wants to
die
She's home alone and no ones around
It's so quiet; she can hear her heart pound
She doesn't feel there is anyone to talk to
She wants to trust someone but doesn't know
who
She decides she won't be lonely anymore
Down in her Dad's room, hidden behind the
door
She holds the shotgun in her hand
The fear inside makes it hard to stand
She goes up to her room and turns on a song
She is happy now even though this is wrong

She sits on her bed
And puts the barrel to her head
A silence falls and a crowd is drawn
The neighbors know something is wrong
Not for her, she's lonely no more
Because of what was hidden behind the door.